Instagram Marketing

How to build a real fan base and market
yourself Social Media Advertising for
beginners Successful on Instagram ... for
step instructions (Edition Instagram)

Aiden Anderson

INSTAGRAM-MARKETING

Create engaging content, attract more followers, and encourage users to interact with your brand

Tips and tricks to be successful on instagram

Instagram is an integral part of everyday life. It is not that long ago that the filters and the typical square format were introduced. Launched in 2010, the app has taken the world by storm. It seems that everyone - including his dog - is now represented on the platform. Now, maybe one or two of you, who used instagram for private purposes, might wonder if social media marketing really is right for their brand. According to statistics, yes: **in the US, 28% of all adults use** instagram and **more than 75% of all instagram users** live outside the US. And with more than **700 million active users per month** the platform has long since made its way into professional life. The feature-rich platform is now used globally, giving organizations the ability to engage and inspire their audiences on a more personal level, finding new employees, and introducing new products.

But instagram is not only used by many users, but also very intense. More than half of all active users (51%) visit the site daily, 35% even several times a day. Originally intended to share photos and videos, the app has quickly become one of the most important social media platforms.

Instagram is great for boosting brand awareness and marketing new products. For example, **70% of**

instagram users have used the platform at least once to find out about a brand. The app allows companies to promote their brands and products in an authentic, engaging way, without being too intrusive.

If you're using instagram for the first time, you may be a little unsure how to do it. No problem, we will help you! A platform like instagram, which is designed for visual content that is also posted in a timely manner, can be a bit intimidating. That's why we've created a comprehensive guide that introduces you step-by-step to the concept of instagram marketing.

If you do not have time to read the complete guide right now, you can just jump to the section that interests you most:

- **create a business profile on instagram**
- **the different types of posts on instagram**
- **create a caption for an instagram post**
- **use hashtags on instagram**
- **develop an instagram marketing strategy**
- **win more instagram followers**
- **tips and tricks for the optimal use of instagram**
- **instagram-analytics**
- **introduction to instagram ads**

CONTENTS

1) CREATE A BUSINESS PROFILE ON INSTAGRAM

First of all, it's important to understand that Instagram is meant to let others share in an experience in real time; H. Share photos and videos right there. It's also critical that you post photos and videos on Instagram on a regular basis because you'll soon forget them. If you do not keep your profile up to date, you'll lose followers and fewer users will interact with your content. Avoid this happening and just follow our tips for making the most of Instagram.

1.1) Download the Instagram app

We recommend that you use the app as Instagram does not currently offer a desktop version that includes all the features of the app. While you may be able to view content on the Instagram website, it is not possible to upload content with the desktop version. The app is available for free from the **Apple App Store** and **Google Play**.

1.2) Create an Instagram account

After you have downloaded the app, you will

create your account in the next step. When you open the app, you'll be offered two options: you can either link your Facebook account or sign in with your phone number or email address. Do not choose your Facebook account here. This would cause your Instagram account to be linked to your personal Facebook profile, and that's something to avoid! Instead, log in with your professional email address.

1.2) Create an Instagram account

After you have downloaded the app, you will create your account in the next step. When you open the app, you'll be offered two options: you can either link your Facebook account or sign in with your phone number or email address. Do **not** choose your Facebook account here. This would cause your Instagram account to be linked to your personal Facebook profile, and that's something to avoid! Instead, log in with your professional email address.

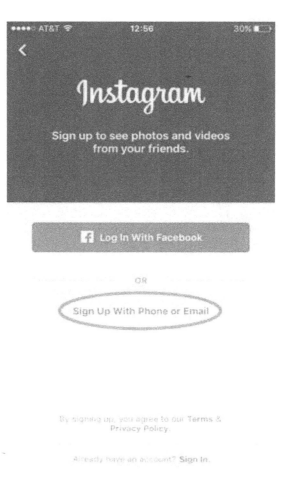

Then enter your data. The name you enter in the "Full name" field does not match your username or alias, but the name that appears in your profile. So choose the name of your business here, so that users can later assign you.

●●●●○ AT&T 📶   13:23   28% 🔋

Name and Password

Add your name so friends can find you.

Cambridge Cheese Shop

●●●●●●●

Next

Already have an account? Sign In.

1.3) Select a user name

In the next step, enter your username. The username is the name of your profile that other Instagram users use when interacting with your brand. Choose a name that users recognize and that is easy to find. If your company name is already taken, just append something to the name so that the first part of your username is definitely the company name. Note: You can change the user name later in the account settings at any time.

1.4) Select a suitable profile picture

Your profile picture is one of the first things a user sees looking for your business on Instagram and viewing your profile. Therefore, it should fit your brand and comply with the guidelines for your company's appearance. A good example would be your logo or a similar, familiar to the users image. Note that the profile picture on Instagram is round and the app automatically crops the photo. Leave enough space at the corners.

•••• AT&T 🛜   14:35   23% ▮▭▸

Add Profile Picture

Add a profile photo so your friends know it's you.

> **Add a Photo**

Skip

●●●●○ AT&T 📶   14:35   ◤ 23% 🔋

Cambridge
Cheese Shop

Add Profile Picture

Change Photo

Next

1.5) Write an appealing description / biography

Before you can publish your first contributions, you must first write your description / biography.

Since you have **a maximum of 150 characters available**, you should formulate as precisely and concisely as possible. Explain to your target group on a personal level what your company produces and what your brand stands for. You can leave out keywords and hashtags here, as the description / biography is not relevant for them.

You can also use your description / biography to prompt users to perform some action - such as using a specific hashtag or visiting your website. On Instagram, you have only one way to insert a clickable URL and to redirect users to an external website, in your description / biography. Many companies adapt this URL over and over again, so that their most recent contribution is always linked. We recommend that you use this link with a tool like Bitly or Goo.gl to shorten and track them so that your description / biography does not clutter and you can figure out how much you're driving traffic to your website or social media campaigns.

●●●○○ AT&T LTE   12:13   86% ▬▬❚

‹   **refinery29**   ···

7,586   **1.5M**   **490**
posts   followers   following

Following   ▾

Refinery29 ◉
News/Media Website
We aim to create a world in which women feel, see,
and claim their power. We are inclusive and
expressive.
You can also find us on @r29fashion.
likeshop.me/refinery29
Followed by **rayna_gabriella**, **renttherunway**, **meemscakes** +
115 more

Email

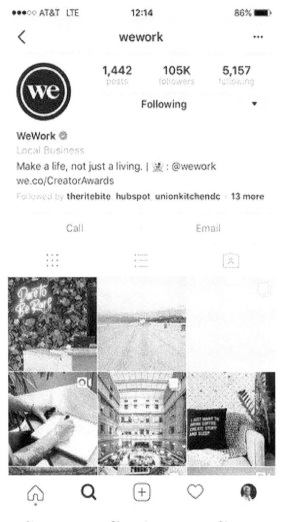

To edit your profile picture, profile name, user name, description / biography or the inserted link, select the "Edit profile" button.

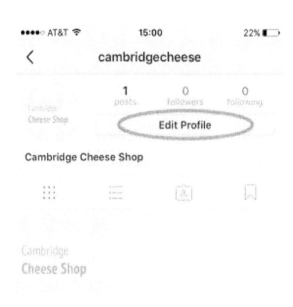

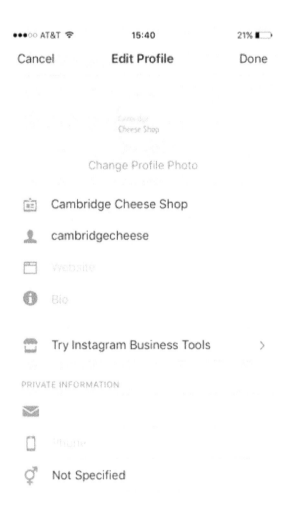

1.6) Adjust your settings

The settings customization menu will open via the small gear (three vertical dots on Android devices) in the top right corner of your profile. Among other things, this menu allows you to change your password, activate notifications, and view all posts that you like "Like." We recommend that you check the following settings immediately:

Story Settings: Here you can specify who your Instagram stories are displayed and who can comment on them. To increase the interaction with your brand as effectively as possible, it is advisable to share your stories with all followers and to allow all followers to add comments.

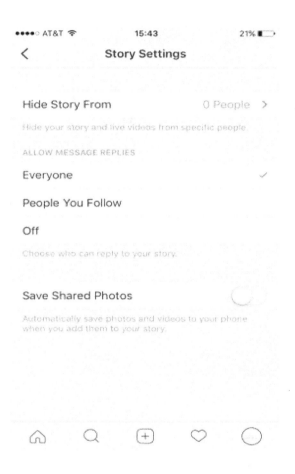

Switch to the Business Profile: Instagram introduced new **business tools** in 2016. These allow companies to present themselves as such, making it easier for users to contact them. Business profiles also provide more granular insights into the performance of content and simplify its optimization. Note: To transform your profile into a business profile, you must have a corporate page on

Facebook.

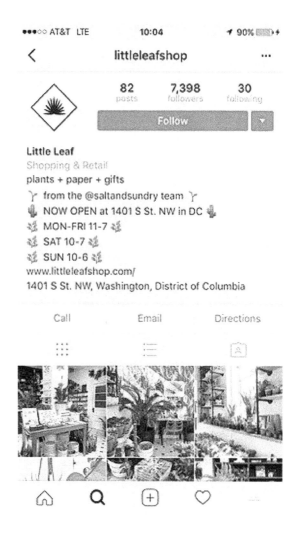

To switch to a business profile, do the following: Open your profile and select the gear icon in the top right to see the settings.

To switch to a business profile, do the following: Open your profile and select the gear icon in the top right to see the settings.

Scroll down and select "Convert to Business Profile."

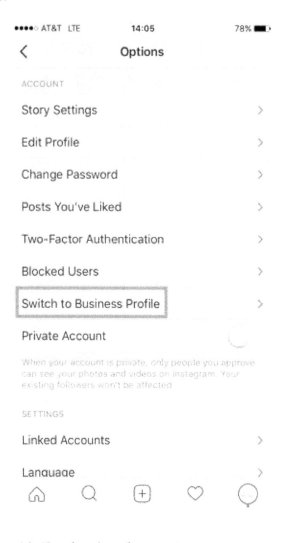

Sign in with Facebook and grant Instagram

administrative access to your pages.

Select the Facebook page you want to link to your Instagram profile. Note: To link the two profiles, you must be an administrator of the Facebook page.

Instagram now imports all relevant data from your

Facebook page. Check them and make any changes.

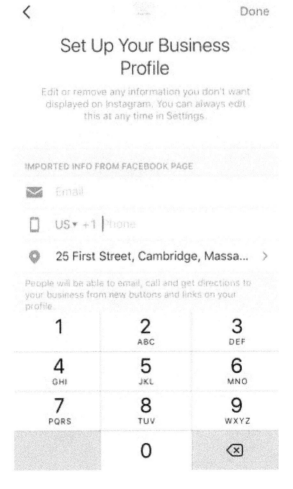

Now you have a business profile on Instagram. Do

not forget to check the profile and account settings.

Private account: Instagram automatically sets up your profile as a public profile. Do not change this! After all, as a business owner, it's up to you to make your posts appear to users automatically, so they can easily follow you.

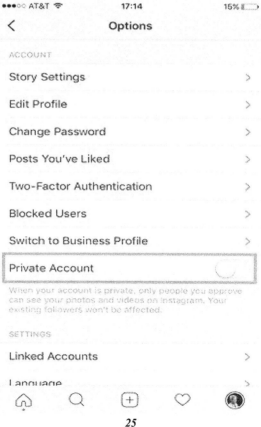

Comments: Most comments on your content will be interesting and motivating. From time to time, however, a comment may violate the values your brand stands for or offend your target audience. In comment settings You can choose to automatically hide comments that contain specific keywords or phrases, such as comments that contain offensive language expressions. Activate the corresponding function and enter the relevant terms and phrases.

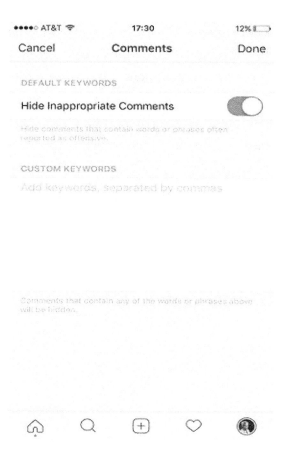

Add more Instagram accounts: If you have multiple Instagram accounts, you can connect them to switch from one to another without having to log out and sign up. You can **add up to five more accounts**, In addition, multiple users can easily log in to the same account at the same time. In this case, you should be sure to keep your editorial calendar up to date so that everyone knows exactly when to post which content. To add an account, open the settings using the gear icon in the top right corner. Scroll down and select "Add account". Enter the user name and password for the account you want to add. To switch to another account, open your profile and tap on the top of your username. You can then choose between all other accounts added.

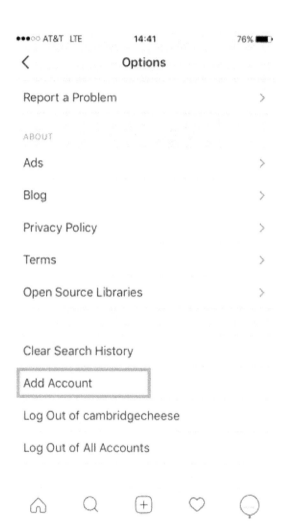

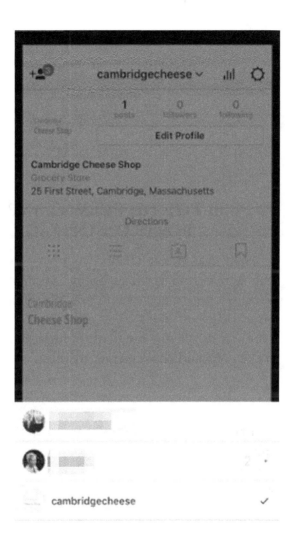

2) THE DIFFERENT TYPES OF POSTS ON INSTAGRAM

Now that you've created your account, it's time to get active and post engaging content. You have various options such as photos, videos and stories at your disposal. Let's take a look at what different types of posts you can post on Instagram and how to make your audience interact the best.

2.1) PHOTOS

Photos are most often shared on Instagram. It is important that you post a colorful mix of different images. Choose photos that showcase your corporate culture and be sure not only to post lifestyle photos, but also to take a look behind the scenes. Also, you should not share too many product photos. Instagram users value authentic corporate contributions, but less obvious ads. Take a look at Nike's Instagram account, for example. Here you will also find photos of Nike products, but mainly pictures of athletes and concerts as well as other content that expresses the personality of the brand.

As you get more involved with the app, you'll find that Instagram offers countless photo subscription options. Here you can let your creativity run wild! We recommend that you take notes when exploring the app when you discover a type of photo that you think fits very well with your brand. To help you get started, here are some of the most successful types of Instagram photo post:

2.1.1) A look behind the scenes

Contributions of this kind are intended to provide your followers with insights into areas of your company that are generally not accessible to the public. The top priority here is authenticity. So make sure that your photos are not posed. A good example of this type of contribution is the photo below of the Aeronaut Brewing Company showing some employees at work.

aeronautbrewing
Aeronaut Brewing Company

...

♡ ⎙ ↪

♥ 69 likes

aeronautbrewing The #AERONAUT foods
hub is a #chocolate #happyplace. Who
wants to lick the spoon? #localfood
#eatlocal #slowfood #somerville

2.1.2) Share posts from employees

Sometimes you find the best content in the profiles of your own employees. If you discover matching photos there, then share them. This is a great way to get authentic content and communicate with your audience on a personal level. Content like this not only encourages your audience to interact with your brand, it also helps build a personal relationship with your employees. For example, the profile of the Fenway Park baseball stadium regularly shares photos showing employees how to repair the stadium prior to the match. Just do not forget to point out who originally published the post.

2.1.3) Informative contributions

This type of post is intended to give users a brief explanation of how to achieve a specific goal. These explanations are in the form of photos or videos and are usually very easy to understand. The popular cooking video series "Tasty" by Buzzfeed is an excellent example of how contributions can be informative and entertaining at the same time.

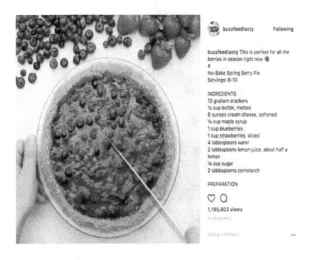

2.1.4) Influencer contributions

Influencer contributions use the reputation of a celebrity or VIP to draw attention to a brand. A star is usually shown here, how he uses a product or interacts with it. One of the benefits of this type of contribution is that you reach a new audience.

The following contribution by Goal Zero shows, for example, the well-known climber and photographer Alex Honnold, who is currently using a solar-powered charger of the brand on the road. With this photo, Goal Zero not only gets the attention of its own target group, but also the more than 499,000 Instagram followers from Honnold.

2.1.5) Inspiring posts

Posts of this type usually consist of simple graphics with a motivational quote or quote in the foreground. These posts are great for inspiring your audience and strengthening your brand value. They are extremely efficient, but should be used with caution, as they can quickly become sentimental. With apps like **Quipio** and **Typic**, you can easily add text to photos and also ensure that the posts meet your brand guidelines.

2.1.6) Share posts of other users

Like your employees' posts, your fans' and followers' posts are a great source of authentic content. Regularly review the posts where you've tagged or used your hashtag. If you find posts there that accurately reflect the values of your brand, you can share them in your profile. Not only is this a compliment to the user who originally posted the post, it also shows that your customers are really important to you. Just do not forget to mention the original author with an @Mention in the caption. To share **someone else's** contribution, you can either take a screenshot and crop it, or you can use a dedicated app like **Repost for Instagram.**

At WeWork, a #DogsOfWeWork campaign is conducted every year . It selects the most successful dog photos posted with this hashtag and adds them to a calendar. Although the WeWork team does not share every photo of their employees on their Instagram profile, the campaign is so well-known that it significantly increases the reach of its posts and significantly increases the interaction rate.

2.1.7) Newsjacking

Nowadays, there seems to be a "holiday" for almost every occasion. Events such as the Sibling Day or the National Ice Cream Day receive a significant amount of attention on social media. Take advantage of this and join local, national and worldwide trends of this kind. This post type is used to post humorous content to events that are basically insignificant.

An example of this is the following post the US restaurant chain Cava Mezze Grill on the occasion of the first baseball game of the season. Here, the Cava Mezze Grill team cleverly used American baseball enthusiasm.

cavagrill   ...

♡ ◯ ↱

♥ 179 likes

cavagrill Happy Nats Season, DC! 🌟

Here's how #34 @bharper3407 fuels up on
game day: White Rice, Chicken, Red Pepper

2.1.8) Recommended sizes for Instagram photos

Compared to the layouts of other social media
profiles, that of an Instagram profile is quite simple.
This inevitably puts the content posted in the
spotlight. Although this promotes interaction, it also
means that quality deficits immediately stand out. Be
sure to share only high-resolution photos on your
Instagram profile. In general, the format is

recommended 1080 × 1080 pixels - so a square. The app also supports the landscape format or an aspect ratio of 1.91: 1. Users only see the photo in this format when they tap the thumbnail. In the feed, the photo will still be displayed as a square and truncated accordingly. In addition, photos in portrait orientation with an aspect ratio of 4: 5 are supported.

2.1.9) Record appealing photos with your smartphone

If you're wondering if you can shoot beautiful, high-quality photos without a professional camera, yes, that's quite possible. The **technology of smart phone cameras** is now so advanced that it can compete with that of expensive, professional cameras. Nowadays you do not have to be a photographer to take professional photos. And you already have the means to do that. The following tips will help you gain more followers and get users to interact more with your brand:

2.1.9.1) Adhere to the "rule of thirds"

In order to align your camera optimally, you should activate the grid view. Then make sure that your object is at a point where a vertical and a horizontal line intersect. This method is called the rule of thirds and was originally used by painters and illustrators. It applies equally to photos. By placing the object of a photo slightly off center, an imbalance arises that makes the photo look more interesting. On an iPhone, you enable the grid view as follows:

Open the settings, choose Photos & Camera, and activate the grid.

2.1.9.2) Focus on a single object

It is sometimes said that the job of a photographer is to find harmony even in chaos. If you scan different objects at the same time and choose a crowded background at the same time, this will distract you from the actual subject of your photo and may even confuse your target audience. Therefore, choose to have only one object per photo and remove any distractions by cutting them out later or by looking at a plain background as you shoot.

2.1.9.3) Use the negative space to your advantage

Negative space is the unused area around the object of a photo. It's important because it makes sure that the photo does not look crowded and the viewer's eye is focused on the subject.

2.1.9.4) Choose interesting perspectives

Often we are used to only one perspective in everyday life - that of our eye level. As a result, National Geographic photographers often choose unusual perspectives, making their photos look interesting and unusual. For example, take photos from high above from a bird's eye view - or even from the bottom, from the perspective of a worm. Try to show familiar objects from a new perspective by trying new angles.

2.1.9.5) symmetry

Our eye perceives symmetrical shapes and objects

as pleasant and harmonious. For symmetrical images, it is usually advisable to omit the rule of thirds and to position your object so that both halves of the photograph are symmetrical. For an even more interesting photo, you can use leading lines that direct the viewer's eye to the subject.

2.1.9.6) template

In addition to symmetrical shapes, we also find patterns as appealing. It can be a tiled floor or a pattern created by nature, such as the individual leaves of a flower or vine on a wall. If you then break this pattern with an object, you get a photo that immediately captivates its viewers.

2.1.9.7) Choose natural light

Electric light from above can create harsh shadows and make certain areas of the photo undesirably dark or bright. Avoid this by always choosing soft natural light whenever possible. For example, take photos near a window that allows diffused light to enter the room. For outdoor shots, the 30 minutes before and after sunrise and sunset are recommended. During this time, the sun, which is only just above the horizon, ensures impressive lighting conditions.

2.1.9.8) Add filters and edit your photos

Some photos just seem so great because they were edited. And you can do that too: Instagram has tools and filters that make it **easy to edit photos** and boost their quality in minutes. Just follow the tips below and your homemade lunch will be like a culinary masterpiece. And so, in just a few steps, an amateur photo becomes a professional photo:

First of all, you should only use successful shots. Unhappily positioned objects or poor lighting conditions can not be eradicated even with the greatest amount of processing. You can also edit your photos with other apps. Snapseed, for example, is a free premium photo editing application that lets you optimize color contrast, apply effects such as the HDR effect, and specifically adjust brightness, contrast, and saturation in specific areas of the photo. VSCO is another popular photo editing app with countless free filters mimicking popular movie roll types.

When you upload an edited photo to Instagram, the app will automatically square the photo. But you can easily return to the original size by tapping the icon with the two expansion arrows at the bottom left of the photo.

After uploading, you can now also apply Instagram filters to the externally edited photo. Just be careful not to overdo it. Because every filter fundamentally changes the picture and gives it a very unique character.

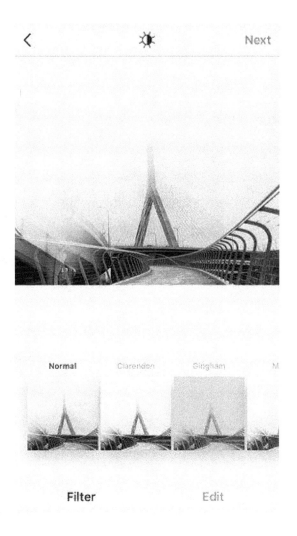

Mayfair

100

Cancel   Done

The next step is to edit your photo using the Lux function. This is according to Instagram, the optimization of the exposure and brightness of photos. It's an effect that makes photos more vibrant and highlights details. You apply the effect by selecting a filter, tapping the sun symbol at the top of the screen, and then adjusting the slider.

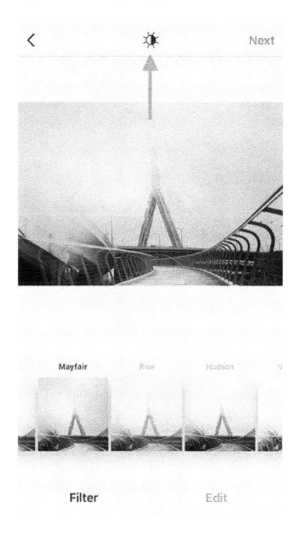

Lux

70

Cancel   Done

Give your photo the finishing touch with Instagram editing tools. Select the "Edit" button and then one of the tools: Alignment, Brightness, Contrast, Structure, etc. When you are ready to publish your photo, select "Next". Fill in the displayed fields and then share your picture.

2.2) VIDEOS

In addition to photos, you can also post videos on

Instagram (up to 60 seconds). You can either upload videos from your computer that have been edited with professional editing software. But you can also choose videos that you've edited yourself using apps. Splice is a popular, free-to-use GoPro editing tool that lets you cut different clips into a video and add transitions, titles, and even music.

When editing videos, keep in mind that they will play on Instagram by default without sound. So make sure that your videos are understood without sound. Or ask users in the caption to turn on the sound. The following video by Purina is a prime example of a successful, entertaining video.

Xem thêm trên Instagram

https://www.instagram.com/p/BDTRNgwweHY
/?utm_source=ig_embed&utm_campaign=embed_v
ideo_watch_again

2.2.1) Boomerangs and GIFs

If you swipe right to Instagram to take a photo, you can choose between Normal, Live, Boomerang, and Hands Free modes. With Boomerangs and GIFs, the traditional video format can be loosened up a bit with repetitive motion sequences and continuous loops. In Boomerang mode, many photos are taken quickly one after the other and then played in continuous loop. This type of post is great for good repeating movements: a person who jumps off something, jarring glasses, or a high five.

2.2.2) Hyperlapse

Hyperlapse Instagram is a separate app that lets you shorten longer videos and optimize them for Instagram. The app offers first-rate time-lapse capability and built-in stabilization technology that lets you play videos absolutely smoothly. To create your own Hyperlapse videos, all you need to do is download the free Hyperlapse app on your mobile device. Agree that the app is allowed to access your camera and you're ready to go. To start recording, tap the round circle - tap again to stop recording. Then you can select the playback speed from 1 to 12 times the speed. Save the hyperlapse video in your gallery and upload it on occasion.

2.2.3) Stories

Instagram stories allow you to post content more often without bombarding your followers or overcrowding your feed. Stories are particularly well suited for behind-the-scenes glimpses and the photos and videos posted here tend to be poorly prepared. Just like Snapchat Stories, Instagram stories are deleted after 24 hours.

Make sure that your content is authentic. While you should post edited photos in your profile feed, your stories may be a little less perfect. Use the feature to give exclusive insights into your brand and your corporate culture. For example, if it's common in your business to bring dogs to the office, stories are just the place to post photos and videos of all the cute dogs in your office. They are also perfect for reporting on live events hosted by your company or in which your team participates.

2.2.4) Create an Instagram story

Instagram offers three different ways to create a story. Touch either the camera icon on the top left, the add story button above your feed, or simply swipe right.

To take a photo, tap and hold the shutter-release button for a video, hold it for a video. As usual, you switch the flash on and off with the flash symbol and switch between the front and rear camera with the arrows.

Give your photo a personal touch. For example, by labeling it with one of the pens. To select a color, simply place your finger on the color you want.

Tap "Aa" to add text or an emoji to your photo using the keyboard. You can select stickers via the smiley face. Swipe left or right to add color filters.

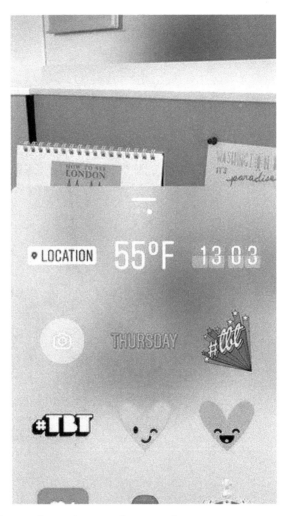

You also have the option **to tag** another **Instagram user** in your story. This is an excellent way to strengthen relationships with other companies and marketing partners. Just type in the @ sign followed by the username of the person or brand you want to tag. If a user now looks at your story, the user name of the selected person or brand will be underlined. If you tap on it, you will be redirected directly to the corresponding profile. If another user mentions you in his story, you will receive a notification.

To publish your story, tap the + icon above "Your Story." Or save the story in your gallery for later posting. After you publish a story, it will appear above your Instagram feed. Alternatively, users can also tap on their profile picture to watch their stories. You can also see who has viewed your story. Open your story and swipe up on it.

As you may have noticed, the story features of Snapchat and Instagram are very similar. Although Snapchat has the advantage of face recognition and various lenses (or filters). But with its broad base of active users and search capabilities, the Instagram app gives businesses a great opportunity to get noticed. So do not hesitate, just use the advantages of the Instagram stories for your company.

2.3) INSTAGRAM LIVE

On Instagram, you can also share videos live with your target audience. To do this, open the app and then the camera. Then select "Live" in the menu at the bottom of the screen and then "Start Live Video". Once you start the live video, any followers that are online will be notified that they can watch your video. The integrated chat feature allows viewers to comment on the live video while streaming. We recommend using this feature sparingly and reserving for live content and live question and answer sessions.

3) CREATE A CAPTION FOR AN INSTAGRAM POST

A picture may sometimes say more than a thousand words, but it does not provide additional context. This - not to be underestimated - purpose fulfills the caption.

But writing good Instagram captions is not easy. Therefore, we have collected some tips for you to help you create meaningful, concise captions.

First of all, you should take enough time for this task. Design different variants and ask friends or colleagues for their opinion. Of course, you should post your content as soon as possible, but more importantly, it is appealing. This is also suggested by the fact that Instagram has changed its algorithm so that users now see the content in their feeds that they are most likely to find interesting. So, the reach of your posts depends on how many "Like" clicks and comments they receive. So it's worth taking the time to create content that will really appeal to your customers.

The length of the caption is also crucial. Instagram has a maximum of 2,200 characters per caption. This is rather long compared to the 140 characters provided by Twitter. Keep in mind, however, that users will initially see only the first three to four lines and they need to actively fade in the rest by tapping "More". So, be sure to mention the most important things first, to make sure that this is displayed in any case. Apart from that, you can take full advantage of the space available. Captions provide an excellent opportunity to provide background information about the posted photo. For example, Humans of New York uses captions to attach quotes from the persons being photographed.

You can also include a call-to-action in your
caption to encourage your audience to like, comment
on, or share your photo with friends. You can also
direct them to the above-mentioned link in your
profile to get them to click and see your new product
or read a new blog post. Be sure to include the
correct link (to your recent post). A tip: Use

shortened tracking URLs so you can track how you increase your traffic with your Instagram activity.

Also, do not forget to add a geo tag. For postings with location markers, **the interaction rate is 79% higher** than for posts without a geo-tag. Adding a location to your post will give users another way to find what you're looking for. And the more users watch your content, the more it interacts with it.

Another key factor is choosing the right style and tone for your Instagram appearance. This may surprise you, but in fact, on every social platform, a different tone is common and appropriate. This means that a phrase can be perfect for Twitter at the same time, but not suitable for Instagram. The best results are usually achieved with contributions that sound casual and authentic. Experiment with emojis and similar tools to personalize your Instagram appearance. Do not be discouraged if you do not succeed right away. It may take a while for you to find the right voice for your brand.

If in doubt, keep your captions short. There is little correlation between the length of the caption and the interaction rate, but short captions increase the meaningfulness of your content.

4) USE HASHTAGS ON INSTAGRAM

Everyone knows them and most of them use them: **hashtags**. The tags originally developed for Twitter are now indispensable in any social network. A hashtag consists of one or more keywords that are strung together without a space and preceded by a hash (#). They are used to assign posts to specific topics such as specific events and conferences or general topics such as pop culture and entertainment etc. They are a great way to increase the reach of posts.

4.1) How to use hashtags on Instagram

Just like all other social media feeds, Instagram feeds are constantly changing. Considering that **over 95 million photos are shared** on the platform **every day**, that's not surprising. For you personally, this huge amount of content means you have to come up with something to stand out from the crowd. And here hashtags come into play.

Hashtags bundles contributions from Instagram users into a single feed that would otherwise be unrelated to each other. If your account is public, your post will be displayed to any user looking for a hashtag that you used in this post.

Instagram's hashtag feeds are fairly simple and designed to make it easy for users to quickly find similar content. Each feed is divided into three sections: Top, Current and Similar. The top-of-the-line section is at the top of a popular hashtag or location feed, and includes the nine posts that are currently the most interacting. Under "Current" you will find a live stream of all posts that have been tagged with the selected hashtag, with the most recent entry always being displayed first. If you choose a currently popular, much used hashtag, your feed will go down the feed very quickly. The Similar section is a great source for finding other hashtags that other users use in the context of this topic.

The use and creation of hashtags is very easy. Just pick any string or sequence of numbers or emojis and add up to 30 hashtags to your caption or comment. And do not forget to make your account public so your posts will appear in hashtag feeds as well.

4.2) Choosing the right Instagram hashtag

As you can see, hashtags have a big impact on your Instagram success. The only question is how to choose the most appropriate hashtags for a post. Look for suitable keywords and current trends directly on Instagram. If you do not have any clues yet, you should first look at the "Search" tab. Tap currently popular posts and see which hashtags have been used.

If you already know which hashtag you would like to use, you can use the Find section to find popular similar hashtags. To do this, tap on the magnifying glass in the menu bar at the bottom and then enter the desired hashtag at the top of the search field. On the "Tags" tab you can check how many posts were marked with your hashtag or similar hashtags.

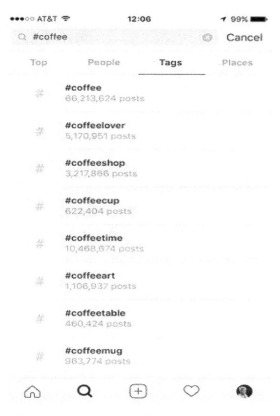

To make sure your contribution is as long-lasting as possible, choose a mix of common, popular, and specific hashtags. In some cases, the creation of a brand-specific hashtag is recommended. For example, some companies have created a new, dedicated hashtag to promote a new product, an Instagram campaign, an event, or similar. In this case, make absolutely sure that your hashtag does not actually exist, and ask your target audience to use your hashtag.

4.3) Position Instagram hashtags correctly

Now that you've found the perfect combination of hashtags for your new post, it's time to decide where to put the hashtags in your content. It is also important here that you do not overdo it. Hashtags should naturally fit into your caption. A study that looked at 100 of the most successful brands on Instagram showed that, on average, they used **only 2.5 hashtags per post**. We recommend that you limit yourself to one to four hashtags per post so as not to overwhelm your target audience.

If you have difficulty integrating the selected hashtags into your caption, just put them at the end of your text or in the first comment. The position of hashtags has no influence on their mode of action. So you do not have to integrate them into the text at all costs.

5) DEVELOP AN INSTAGRAM MARKETING STRATEGY

You may feel like many others: you know how important it is to be present on Instagram, you want to be active on the platform, but you do not know how to do it the best way. Many companies are forced to advertise their brand on any social network, and they do not take enough time to work out a sophisticated strategy. Since Instagram is quite different from all other social networks, this platform requires a very **individual marketing strategy**. The tips below will help you to find your own personal style for your Instagram appearance.

5.1) Determine your Instagram audience

As with any other platform, you should first determine which audience you want to target. If you already have other marketing strategies, you can use them as a foundation. Then narrow your Instagram audience by setting the following factors: age, location, gender, income, interests, goals, and typical challenges.

but how does it continue? Keep track of popular hashtags on events and topics that are relevant to your business. Find out who's using and interacting with these hashtags and look at the profiles of these Instagram users. You can also look closely at the followers of a competitor. Sometimes it's actually easier than you think to choose your target audience.

5.2) Conduct a competitive analysis

After determining your Instagram audience, you should run a competitive analysis to find out what content your competitors are posting on Instagram. If you already know who your main competitors are, look at their Instagram profiles. If not, you can find similar company profiles by entering search terms that are relevant to your business or industry. Then check what your competitors' contributions get the most attention, which popular hashtags are used, how the captions are designed, how often posts are published, and how successful the companies are. This information will then help you to design and optimize your own Instagram profile.

If you notice in the analysis of the contents of your competitors that they missed a certain chance so far, make a note of them. Because with new content you can stand out from the crowd.

5.3) Set up an editorial calendar

On average, **six photos per week** Posted by companies, that is more than 300 pictures a year. With this amount it is not easy to keep track of which content has already been published and which posts should be posted and when. Here's an editorial calendar to help you significantly reduce the administrative burden of your Instagram account. In this calendar, you can sort your posts by post type (see above), design your captions and hashtags, and create a schedule for posting each post. In addition, the editorial calendar is a great way to capture important events that you want to get noticed on Instagram - such as the launch of a new product or a discount promotion. **Without an editorial calendar** It can happen that you are so busy looking for content ideas that you do not have time to look for current opportunities.

5.4) Pay attention to a uniform brand appearance

If you randomly post content and your posts do not match, you'll confuse your audience and likely lose followers. Therefore, it is important that you find a clear line and pay attention to a uniform brand appearance. It helps to think about your brand personality. What are your brand values? Would you like to present it cheeky, playful, direct or bold?

For example, the lifestyle and interior design experts at **Apartment Therapy** have used the popular concept #foodporn (the appealing presentation of delicious food) in apartments. The brand stands for bright, immaculate, well-structured furnishing concepts and this is exactly what the Instagram presentation of Apartment Therapy reflects. Ideally, a user recognizes at first glance that a photo in their feed comes from you.

Another excellent example of a successful unified presentation of the brand personality is Taco Bell.

The company has adapted its feed to the more outspoken style and on-the-go lifestyle of Millennials, its target audience, and focuses on entertaining photo contributions to encourage users to interact.

Once you've defined your brand personality, you can start aligning your content with it. This may even affect the color picker for photos.

Also, focus your posts on the story you want to tell about your brand. Capturing interesting captions in captions helps build a personal relationship between you and your audience. A good example of successful storytelling is **Red Bull's** feed, which contains countless photos and videos of challenging sports situations.

5.5) Convert Instagram followers to customers

Once you have built a solid base of followers, you can take initial action to convert these to paying customers. The following options are available, among others:

1. Promotions: Promotions, discounts, "Two for the price of one" promotions and similar promotions are great for getting Instagram users up and running for the first time. Make sure you clearly state the terms of the offer and point to the end date of the action to give some urgency.

2. Competitions: One of the most effective ways to attract new customers is to provide a trial version of your product. As part of the contest, challenge users to follow you on Instagram or tag a post with a specific hashtag.

3. Social engagement: According to a recent survey, 81% of companies millennials expect public commitment to engage socially. This means that with social engagement, you can increase your brand affinity and your chances of converting followers to customers. An example of this is the fashion label Gap, which supports the organization The Global Fund in the fight against AIDS in Africa. Gap has helped raise more than $ 130 million since 2006.

4. Teaser: Instagram is perfect for giving your target audience first glimpses of new, upcoming products. But be careful not to flood the feeds of your followers with pure product photos. Post only one or the other photo and thus arouse the curiosity of the users.

5. Live Launch of Products: In some cases, it's a good idea to give users the ability to track the launch of a product in real time via Instagram Live. You can also encourage viewers to buy directly by inserting a link into their profile to purchase their new product.

6) WIN MORE INSTAGRAM FOLLOWERS

Your content is created and matching hashtags are selected. But **how do you know that more Instagram users are following you?** Gaining more followers is a costly undertaking for any business, whether it's an established business with thousands of followers or a recently formed company. Do not be tempted to choose the easy way and buy followers. Because these followers do not interact with your content. This means that later you will miss the interactions that would ensure that your posts appear in users' feeds. Instead, follow the tips below to gain more followers in a sustainable way.

First of all, you should **have chosen a user name, recognize the user and make it easy to find.** If you are not found, you will not be able to follow ... Next, optimize your profile. Keep in mind that the profile is the last one users read before deciding whether to follow you. Be sure to specify who you are and what you offer.

Once your profile is ready, you can post your first posts. It's a good idea to post a few posts (15 or more) before you actively engage with more interactions and followers. Because if users want to look at your profile but find no content there, they probably will not follow you. Since you only have a few posts at the beginning, you should definitely pay attention to the highest quality. **For while Facebook or Twitter followers quite forgive one or the other misstep, Instagram followers are much stricter here**. A single bad photo can already have far-reaching consequences.

After you have published some contributions yourself, you should start following other users that interest you and that are related to your business. Consider Instagram as a community. Connect with other companies in your area or influencers who might be interested in your product / service. If you choose to follow a user, you will immediately interact with their content as well. This is a great way to draw attention to your own profile without being intrusive. If you interact with another user's content or decide to follow the profile, that user will receive a notification. This will then cause the user to hopefully **Be sure to show your followers that you value them. You do this by responding to their comments and interacting with their content.**

Encourage other Instagram users to share your content. Ask your brand ambassador to recommend your profile, or partner with similar companies. For example, a small shop could work with a well-known stylist to raise awareness of current seasonal trends.

Do not forget to promote your Instagram profile on other channels. **Allow visitors to your site to share content on Instagram,** or encourage followers on other social networks to follow you on Instagram. Sometimes, the fastest way to get new followers is simply by asking.

7) 6 TIPS AND TRICKS FOR OPTIMAL USE OF INSTAGRAM

Now that you know the most important things about using Instagram, we'd like to share some tips that not everyone knows, but that will help you get the most out of the platform. As the instructions refer to the latest version, we recommend that you update your version before proceeding.

7.1) The perfect time for an Instagram post

Since Instagram is a mobile app, its users are active throughout the day. However, you can increase the interaction with your content by publishing content to **Instagram at specific times**. It's best to post content on a Monday or Thursday at any time, except between 3pm and 4pm (local time of your audience). Experience shows that Instagram users tend to interact with content on weekdays and outside work hours.

7.2) Link your Instagram profile to your Facebook page

One of the peculiarities of Instagram is that the app allows users to seamlessly share content on other social platforms. Even if it makes sense to automatically link your other social media profiles (Facebook or Twitter), we advise against it. Because content that brings good results on Instagram does not necessarily do so on other platforms. It's important to focus your content on each platform. However, of course, your posts will get more attention if you link your Instagram profile to your other social media accounts, such as your Facebook page. Note: If you've set up a business profile on Instagram, your Facebook page is already linked to it.

If you decide to link your Instagram profile and

your Facebook page, all you have to do is follow a few simple steps: Open your Instagram profile and tap the gear in the top right corner. In the Options menu, scroll down to the settings and look for "Linked Accounts." If you have not signed up for Facebook on your mobile device yet, you are now being asked to do so. Then select the Facebook company page to link to. You will then be directed to the "Share Settings". If the Facebook logo is blue, content sharing on Facebook is enabled.

7.3) Show posts marked as "Like"

Instagram offers the ability to view all posts that you've previously marked as "Like" by going to the "Options" menu of your profile. Tap the gear icon and select "Posts you like." Here you can Now you can search all marked photos and videos.

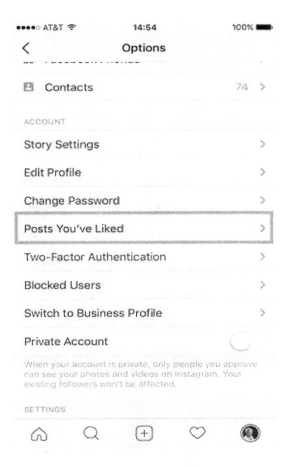

7.4) Rearrange Instagram Filter

In order to be able to upload photos faster in the future, Instagram offers the possibility to position your most frequently used filters first in the filter selection. To rearrange the filters or hide certain filters, open a post to edit it. When the filters appear, scroll to the far right and tap the gear icon under

Manage. Place your finger on the three gray lines to the left of a filter and drag it up or down to the desired location. If you want to hide a filter, just remove the check mark to the right of the filter.

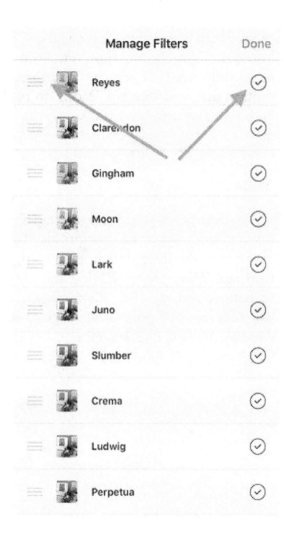

7.5) Insert line breaks in captions

You may also have noticed that when writing a caption on Instagram the Enter key or Enter key on the keyboard is suddenly missing. You can easily show them again by tapping the 123 key.Before inserting a line break, however, keep in mind that users only need to see the first three lines of the caption first, and then tap "More" to read all the text. So be sparing with line breaks.

7.6) Hide posts in which you have been marked

To view posts you've tagged, tap the person icon on the bottom right of your profile. To remove such a post, tap the three dots in the top right corner and then tap "Hide photos". Select the photos you want to remove and tap Hide Photos again. Note that this will only remove posts from your profile. They will continue to exist on Instagram.

If you want to bypass this step, you can also set flags to appear in your profile only if you have agreed to it. To do this, tap the three dots again and then tap Marking Options. Select the option "Add manually" here. Now you will be informed each time you have been marked in a post. To see the post in your profile, tap the photo and then tap View in my profile.

Instagram Marketing (Aiden Anderson)

Options   Done

PHOTOS OF YOU

Choose how you want photos of you added to your profile.

Add Automatically

Add Manually   ✓

Learn more about Photos of You

8) INSTAGRAM-ANALYTICS

Unlike Facebook, Instagram does not yet offer the possibility to perform detailed analyzes within the app. After switching to a business profile, however, there are some simple analysis functions available. To get statistics on the number of followers and impressions, the reach of posts, and interactions. To do so, tap "Show insights" below your uploaded photo or video. With Facebook's Ad Manager, you can also keep track of the number of impressions and interactions, as well as the cost of ad campaigns. While these statistics provide some helpful information. However, as they only ever refer to a specific post or campaign, they do not provide a comprehensive overview.

But there are a few third-party apps that help you analyze your Instagram content in more detail. With Iconosquare and Simply Measured, you can track other metrics, such as the growth in followers and the increase in interactions over time. You can determine the ideal time to publish content based on the performance of previous posts, and compete with selected competitors. Both apps are chargeable. However, you can first load a trial version to check if the app meets your analysis requirements.

Which Instagram metrics are important to you always depends on your individual goals. But some basic metrics should keep an eye on every business. These include interactions (likes and comments) and the growth of followers over time. When you post content that adds value to your audience, you'll automatically gain more and more followers, and get more likes, comments, and video views with future posts. Even if you do not really need any detailed insights or you do not have enough budget for better analytics tools, it's important to keep track of these basic metrics. Because only then can you make sure. Unlike Facebook, Instagram does not yet offer the possibility to perform detailed analyzes within the app. After switching to a business profile, however, there are some simple analysis functions available. To get statistics on the number of followers and impressions, the reach of posts, and interactions. To do so, tap "Show insights" below your uploaded photo or video. With Facebook's Ad Manager, you can also keep track of the number of impressions and interactions, as well as the cost of ad campaigns. While these statistics provide some helpful information. However, as they only ever refer to a specific post or campaign, they do not provide a comprehensive overview.

But there are a few third-party apps that help you analyze your Instagram content in more detail. With Iconosquare and Simply Measured, you can track other metrics, such as the growth in followers and the increase in interactions over time. You can determine the ideal time to publish content based on the performance of previous posts, and compete with selected competitors. Both apps are chargeable. However, you can first load a trial version to check if the app meets your analysis requirements.

Which Instagram metrics are important to you always depends on your individual goals. But some basic metrics should keep an eye on every business. These include interactions (likes and comments) and the growth of followers over time. When you post content that adds value to your audience, you'll automatically gain more and more followers, and get more likes, comments, and video views with future posts. Even if you do not really need any detailed insights or you do not have enough budget for better analytics tools, it's important to keep track of these basic metrics. Because only then can you make sure.

9) INTRODUCTION TO INSTAGRAM ADS

If you've been posting engaging content regularly and building a base of loyal followers, the time has come to worry about advertising on Instagram. Being able to advertise on Instagram provides companies with a unique opportunity to interact with their buyer persona. Since Instagram ads are simply shown to users as more posts in their feed, they are less noticeable and annoying than typical ads. They allow you to naturally motivate your audience to learn more about your business and product.

9.1) Create an Instagram ad

You can create an Instagram ad much like a Facebook ad, because Instagram ads are created using the Facebook Ad Manager.

In the first step, either select the Instagram post whose performance you want to improve, or create a new ad using the Facebook Ad Manager. If this is the first ad you create on Facebook, you'll be asked to create an ad account. You'll also need to link your Instagram business profile to your Facebook page.

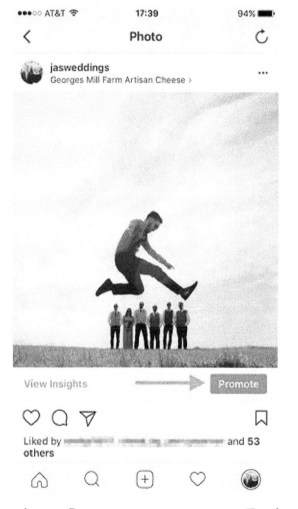

To assign an Instagram account to your Facebook page, visit the Business Manager. Hover over the menu on the left and select the "Instagram

Accounts" option. Then select the option to assign an Instagram account. Enter the details of your account and select "Continue."

Select a campaign goal and name the campaign. Note that only a few of the destinations that can be selected on Facebook will have the option for Instagram ads. These include the following goals:

- Brand awareness
- reach
- Traffic
- App installs
- interactions
- video Views
- Conversions

After deciding on a marketing goal, name the ad group.

Name der Anzeigengruppe DE - 18+   Erweiterte Optionen

If you have selected the "Traffic" destination, you

will be prompted to specify a traffic destination. Here you have the choice between a website and an app.

The next step is to define the audience for your ad by specifying demographic and psychographic data. These include age, gender, location, language, workplace, financial status, patterns of behavior, and connections. If you have already saved custom audiences, you can also choose from them here.

Zielgruppe
Lege fest, wer deine Werbeanzeigen sehen soll. Mehr dazu

Neu erstellen Gespeicherte Zielgruppe verwenden ▼

Custom Audiences ⓘ Custom Audiences oder Lookalike Audiences hinzufügen

Ausschließen Neu erstellen ▼

Standorte ⓘ Jeder an diesem Ort ▼

Deutschland

♀ Deutschland

♀ Einschließen ▼ Füge andere Standorte ein Durchsuchen

Standorte auf einmal hinzufügen

Alter ⓘ 18 ▼ - 65+ ▼

Geschlecht ⓘ Alle Männer Frauen

Sprachen ⓘ Gib eine Sprache ein

Detailliertes Targeting ⓘ Personen EINSCHLIESSEN, auf die mindestens EINES der folgenden Merkmale zutrifft ⓘ

Demografie, Interessen oder Verhaltensweisen Vorschläge Durchsuchen

Personen ausschließen

Weitere die Interessen aus, wenn diese die Link-Klicks zu geringeren Kosten pro Link-Klick steigern könnte ⓘ

Verbindungen ⓘ Verbindungsart hinzufügen ▼

Diese Zielgruppe speichern

After you define your audience, in the Placements section, choose Edit Placements and choose Instagram as the platform. Attention! If you forget this step, your ad will only appear on Facebook. If you only want your ad to run on Instagram, make

113

sure none of the other platforms are selected.

The next step is to set your budget and the time in which your ad will show. Here you can choose between "daily budget" and "runtime budget" and define the start and end date of your campaign. If you do not specify a start and end date, or set a runtime budget, your ad will run permanently and the selected daily budget will apply. Use the View Advanced Options drop-down menu to access additional budget and schedule settings. For example, here you can set the ad to be activated only at certain times of the day. It also gives you faster results if you choose the Accelerated option. This option is especially useful for advertisements for events that take place in a timely manner.

Next, select the content of your ad. Here you can opt for an existing post to improve its results, or upload a new captioned photo to use as an ad. On Instagram, you have the following options for ads: "Single image", "Single video", "Carousel" or you can sponsor a story ad as part of your Instagram stories. For best results, **Facebook recommends** the following formats: For square ads, you should choose 600x600 pixels image size, 600x315 pixels landscape viewers, and 600x750 pixels portrait size ads. In addition, Facebook advises to keep the text of photo and video thumbnails short.

Once your ad has been uploaded, you can complete the job and start your first Instagram campaign.

9.2) Reasonable budget for Instagram ads

How much you spend on an Instagram ad depends on the goal of your campaign. For example, if you want to earn more leads, you should consider what the cost per lead is and how it relates to the costs on other channels or your customer lifetime value (LTV). This is different in every business and every industry. The same goes for other goals like increasing website clicks and revenue. Regardless of your goal, you should keep an eye on the performance of your Instagram ads and use every opportunity to make the most of your budget.

10) CONCLUSION

With 700 million active users per month, there's no doubt about the reach and impact of Instagram. What used to be a fairly simple photo-sharing app today provides an attractive user experience, including the ability to get a full picture of a company and its brand image.

Keep in mind that Instagram users value high-quality content. Post photos and videos that will provide your audience with interesting information and present your brand in a new, unique way. Optimize your content with entertaining captions that encourage interaction.

The idea of designing and maintaining a platform where you primarily present your brand with visual content may seem a bit intimidating at first. But do not let that put you off - thanks to Instagram this is easy and fun. Find your optimal Instagram marketing strategy! Just follow our tips and let yourself from other companies **inspire**.

Author

-- Aiden Anderson --
Content Strategy Instagram

If this book is useful for you, please **COMMENT POSITIVELY** for **5 STARS** for it, sincerely thank you!
I will update it regularly to provide more value for everyone.

Thank you again very much!